DIVA:
The Handbook

An eight week daily devotional for young women

By: LaKeisha Entsuah

Printed in the United States of America
ISBN-13:978-0692589984
First Printing, 2015

The Aliel Company
Lansdale, PA 19446

info@thedivaseries.com
www.thealielcompany.com

Dedication

I dedicate this book to every young woman who finds it difficult to apply God to real life. To the one who is unsure of her purpose and to the one who is searching for more than what the world is offering.

To my daughter and sister, living proof that my purpose is to nurture the next generation of godly women. To my husband, the awesome man of God who proudly walks this journey with me. To my parents, family and friends, the ones who do more than cheer me on, they pray me on!

Contents

Why DIVA

The term diva is often associated with a sassy, demanding and temperamental woman. She is seen as someone who views herself as above others and behaves as if everyone should cater to her needs. Often celebrities are referred to as Divas for their behavior and their treatment of those around them. For you as a young woman these women, good, bad or indifferent, are prominent role models in society. It is time to reconsider what it means to be a Diva. Instead of allowing you to follow the example of people you may never meet; it is time to teach you how God defines a DIVA.

So why DIVA? There are many words in the English language to choose from, so why one with such negative connotations in today's society. Instead of asking why, you should ask why not. Why not question how the world views us as women? Why not challenge the expectations of success for you as a young woman? God's design for women is so much more than what our society encourages. It is so much deeper than the limits of media images and the idolization of celebrities.

We were created for more than what society expects. Diva is the perfect word to use as we seek to redefine the way you see yourself and how the world sees you.

Our society is full of images which challenge your understanding of who God has called you to be. So many young women fail to realize their value is greater than any material possession on earth. They also fail to realize the great responsibility placed upon us women to be leaders. We've lost accountability to each other in the pursuit of acceptance and superiority. To be better than the one next to me is more important than walking my unique path of greatness. Respectable women are not selfish. Women of God do not harbor jealousy and envy in their hearts. These character traits are what the world expects of us. However they are contrary to what God expects of us.

It is time to challenge the current frame of reference when we use the word Diva. Make her someone to be celebrated and not degraded. Let's create divas other young women aspire to be, not someone they envy or despise. The qualities of God's Diva are qualities which groom her into the coveted Proverbs 31 woman. The qualities of a good leader, mother and wife are the qualities this handbook aims to teach you. At the end of this journey you will see how being a DIVA is an admirable quality. You will realize that God created you to be a DIVA.

D.I.V.A.
Qualities

There are four qualities that create our new definition of DIVA; Discipline, Integrity, Value and Ambition. These qualities are the foundation for godly living. A true diva will embody these qualities and live them daily. She will allow her light to shine in a dark world; she will inspire her peers to become a diva. She will meditate on the scriptures illustrating each quality and abide by them as she navigates life. By her example the term diva will gain new inspiration.

Discipline

Discipline is the first quality of God's Diva. For us to accomplish our goals, we must be disciplined in all we do. We also require discipline or correction from others to help keep us on the right path. We often look at discipline or correction as a negative thing. However, we should see discipline as a necessary tool to ensure we are following God's commands and have not deviated off our path. Though many of us think that our parents made it up, Proverbs 13:24 says "He who spares his rod hates his son." They didn't make it up as an excuse to punish us; they are carrying out a divine commandment.

Integrity

By definition integrity means to be of good moral standing. A diva with integrity lives her life in such a way that no one can speak ill against her for if they do; as 1Peter 3:16 says "they will be ashamed when they see what a good life you live". Your heart guides your ways so it must be of right standing or your actions will contradict your speech. A diva lives an upright life, doing what is right with love and sincerity.

Value

If you want to live an upright life you must know your value. Not as the world defines value but as God defines it. The price paid for your life is too valuable to be squandered away with the standard of living glorified in our society. As 1 Corinthians 6:20 tells us, we were "purchased with a high price". So you must honor God with your body. Our value lies in knowing who you are and whose you are. Understand, you cannot be bought or sold by man; you are to be cherished as a rare gem. God views you as his most precious creation. Why would you not view yourself the same way?

Ambition

One's interpretations of ambition can vary depending on the heart of the individual. The bible speaks often about the dangers of selfish ambition. It warns of the consequences we will face when we become wrapped up in ourselves. It is those times when our own success becomes more important than doing the will of God. On the other hand, there is godly ambition or the desire to live a life pleasing to God. Work daily to make sure all you do is pleasing in his sight. This is what will lead us to the wonderful life God has promised us.

D.I.V.A. Training

Each day we must strive to be a better version of ourselves. We must work to display the diva qualities. This eight week journey will walk you through each quality, ingraining them into your heart and teaching you to use them as daily. Each quality is broken down into two weeks of study. Each week will focus on a different facet of that quality and what the bible says about it. You will notice there are only six days of study in each week for the bible says on the seventh day he rested. Your assignments will consist of the following components.

Weekly Mantra

Each week of study features a mantra that should be recited daily. Allow these thoughts to manifest themselves into your heart and become a part of your belief system. If you allow these words to take root in your mind, it will cause a shift in your outlook of the world. The mantra serves as positive reinforcement of the concepts you will study.

Passage of Mediation

Each week a passage is selected to help you fully understand the concepts outlined in this book. After reading each passage, take time to journal your thoughts and insights. By recording your thoughts about the passage and the overall focus of the week, you will be able to identify how they fit into your life.

Prayer

Prayer and meditation are essential part of your walk with God. They are also essential to basic survival in this crazy world. Your weekly prayer focus should be an addition to your daily prayers as it will help you to further meditate on the lesson for the week. These prayers are also there to help you focus your conversation with God.

Verse of the day

Each day for the next eight weeks there is a verse of reflection centered on the DIVA quality of the week. Each verse provides you with a specific biblical reference for each quality. They are your biblical instructions. The explanation that follows will help you put the verse into practical context.

Reflection

An important part of the growth process is spending time to reflect on your own life and how the concepts apply to you. Each day ends with a proposition for you to examine your own life as it relates to the qualities of a DIVA.

DIVA Challenge

Each week you are assigned a new challenge to help you put the quality of focus into practice. Complete your challenge at the end of the week once you have studied the principle.

Week 1: Accepting Discipline

I can accept Discipline with grace and humility!

When you understand how important discipline is in your life, it allows you to take correction and apply it as a lesson instead of seeing it as an attack against you. Discipline is often needed for your own protection. It comes from a place of love and concern rather than malice. The role of a parent is a divine assignment and there are specific guidelines outlined throughout scripture on how to carry out this assignment. Your job as a child is to honor your mother and father and as they fulfill their divine assignment as your parent. Understand their position as your guide through life and their purpose to raise you up according to God's will. If there are to fulfill their position and purpose they must discipline you.

When you learn to accept discipline, it is not about taking your lumps and not talking back when you are punished. It is about seeing the benefit in having someone who cares enough to alert you when you stray off your path. These warning are not reserved for your parents, yet it is the duty of your entire village to ensure you remain on the right path. The scriptures you will read this week display the consequences of not heeding to discipline.

Passage of Meditation: Hebrews 12:4-11 MSG

In this all-out match against sin, others have suffered far worse than you, to say nothing of what Jesus went through – all that bloodshed! So don't feel sorry for yourselves. Or have you forgotten how good parents treat children, and that God regards you as his children? My dear child, don't shrug off God's discipline, but don't be crushed by it either. It's the child he loves that he disciplines; the child he embraces, he also corrects. God is educating you; that's why you must never drop out. He's treating you as dear children. This trouble you're in isn't punishment; it's training, the normal experience of children. Only irresponsible parents leave children to fend for themselves. Would you prefer an irresponsible God? We respect our own parents for training and not spoiling us, so why not embrace God's training so we can truly live? While we were children, our parents did what seemed best to them. But God is doing what is best for us, training us to live God's holy best. At the time, discipline isn't much fun. It always feels like it's going against the grain. Later, of course, it pays off handsomely, for it's the well-trained who find themselves mature in their relationship with God.

Prayer

Dear heavenly Father, help me to accept the guidance and discipline of those who love me. I understand that they do so for my benefit and not to do me harm. Allow me to take the words of correction and apply them to my life to be a guiding hand along the path you set me on. Thank you God, for those that you place in my life who seek to nurture me and teach me your ways.

Reflections

Take some time to reflect on this week's focus. Keep a journal for any thoughts, questions, and concerns that may arise while reading. You should also take some time to reflect and journal after each day's reading. You may want to journal prayer requests that come to mind after your reading this week's lesson.

DIVA Challenge #1

Write a letter to your parents thanking them for a time when they disciplined you. Explain the lesson you learned from that experience and ask them to respond to your letter by explaining the lesson they intended to teach you through discipline.

_____

_____

_____

_____

_____

_____

_____

_____

_____

_____

_____

_____

Day 1

"Those who spare the rod of discipline hate their children.
Those who love their children care enough to discipline them,"
Proverbs 13:24

Instead of being angry with your parents or other authority figures for disciplining you; consider how much they must love you to take the time and energy to correct you when you are wrong. It is ok for you to be upset or uncomfortable while being disciplined. However, the next time you face it, consider your reaction.

Consider who you are angry with. Is your anger or disappointment directed at the person of authority for punishing you or are you angry with yourself for ending up in this particular situation? When you take the time to identify the source of your disappointment, you may find the person of authority is not the problem. You may also begin to see love in behind the punishment. You may realize their actions were for your benefit.

Reflect on past behaviors you received discipline for; what was the benefit of you not being allowed to continue on the wrong path? Try to focus on the positives of the situation. They may be difficult to find however, they do exist.

Notes of Reflection

_____

_____

_____

_____

_____

_____

_____

Day 2

"To learn you must love discipline; it is stupid to hate correction," Proverbs 12:1

During the learning process you never get every question correct on the first try. Each wrong answer requires correction by your teacher and it is accompanied by and explanation for why you were wrong. Without that correction and explanation, you would never master the concept. With each try you gain a better understanding and with each wrong answer your path to the correct answer becomes clearer.

The same idea applies to discipline for your actions. If you do not receive correction, you will never learn and without explanation, you will never fully understand. With each situation comes wisdom; this wisdom will serve you well throughout life. When you face discipline, God is always willing to help guide you to a place of understanding; you just have to be willing to seek him.

Reflect on something you were able to learn because you listened to the instruction and correction of a teacher or parent. Would you have been able to learn that concept if you had not accepted their correction when you were wrong?

Notes of Reflection

_____

_____

_____

_____

_____

_____

_____

_____

Day 3

"But if you turn away and refuse to listen you will be devoured by the sword of your enemies; I the lord have spoken,"
Isaiah 1:20

You do not have to be in the wrong to benefit from an elder's wisdom and experiences. It can also be an attempt to prevent you from heading down the wrong path. Learning from the experiences of others is like reading the caution signs on the highway. It keeps you from falling into the hole up the road. You are able to see what lies ahead and gain insight into how to handle the situation.

Failing to listen can lead to devastating consequences. There is a benefit to having someone with experience offer you advice. They are saving you the trouble of repeating their mistakes. Understand that you will make mistakes in life. There are times when you will fail, however if you can avoid trials by listening to the wisdom of someone else, you should.

Reflect on a time you received advice to prevent you from heading down the wrong path. What were the consequences of your decision to ignore the advice?

Notes of Reflection

_____

_____

_____

_____

_____

_____

_____

_____

_____

Day 4

"No discipline is enjoyable while it is happening- it is painful!
But afterward there will be a peaceful harvest for those who are
turned in this way." Hebrews 12:11

Just because you must learn to gracefully accept discipline and humble yourself to the process does not mean it will be painless. No form of discipline is enjoyable; no one looks forward to being chastised for doing something wrong. Despite the initial pain involved, the benefits far outweigh the drawbacks. Instead of focusing on what you lost, reflect on what you will gain from each experience.

The dreams you have for your life are more likely to come to fruition if you take heed to the discipline you receive. Use it as a stepping stone to the next level in your journey. Without it you may never get to where you wish to go. When you consider what you stand to gain by learning this lesson now, it should make accepting the discipline easier to bear. View discipline as a gift for the future rather than a punishment for right now.

Think of ways to focus on the possible positive outcomes of being disciplined and learning a lesson. Consider the things you will gain by not heeding to the influences of the world.

Notes of Reflection

_____

_____

_____

_____

_____

Day 5

"For their command is a lamp and their instruction a light; their corrective discipline is a way of life." Proverbs 6:23

Each of us needs guidance; you need someone to show you the way. God is our ultimate guide. He lays out a plan for your life way before your parents even considered conceiving you. Along your life's journey, God places people in your path to help guide you. These people are there to help us stay on our divine path. They are like the annoying voice in the GPS that yells at you when you make a wrong turn. We love having the GPS so we don't get lost. But, when we fail to listen carefully to instruction we get frustrated with its response.

The people God places in your life have part of the map you need to get through life. They know where each path leads. If you wander down the wrong path they will bring you back into the fold. Imagine if your guide allowed you to continue to wander down the wrong path. Where would you end up; what type of life would you live?

Take an inventory of the people in your life; reflect on the ways they have helped you along your journey. What correction have they provide to help get you to where you are today?

Notes of Reflection

_____

_____

_____

_____

_____

_____

Day 6

"Discipline you children while there is hope; otherwise you will ruin their lives." Proverbs 19:18

There is a reason you received a time out at age two, had toys taken away at 9 and grounded at 12. Your parents were trying to help you to understand that the older you get and the more serious your "crimes" are, the harsher your punishments will become. Your parents hope that if they disciplined you at home it will help you to understand the severity of your actions. Therefore, when you get out into the world you will obey the laws to avoid the consequences.

At the present moment you see your punishment as an attempt to ruin your life. Punishment is often a blow to your social persona or a downgrade in your level of cool. However, the punishment serves to save your life from ruin. When you feel you are exempt from punishment, you tend to have less respect for rules.

Consider the consequences of committing a crime in the real world. Reflect on pass punishments that will now prevent you from committing such crimes. What have you learned from those situations that help keep you on the right path?

Notes of Reflection

_____

_____

_____

_____

_____

_____

Week 2: Self-Discipline

I am in complete control of my actions. I choose to live according to the word of God

---

Self-discipline or self-control is more about choices than about ability. Each of us can practice self-control; it is a choice to do wrong. You can stay out past curfew or go home at the appropriate time. You can walk away from a potentially bad situation. You can also not to walk into situation that may bring you trouble. The real difference between those who seem to get it right those who don't is a choice.

However, even for those who make the choice, their ability to be steadfast in those decisions must be practiced daily. Otherwise they risk being swayed by the enemy. You will often hear older people say the devil made me do it. The truth is the devil presented you with an option. Your lack of self-discipline allowed you to accept his offer. God has given us free will and with that comes the responsibility to practice our ability to resist temptation. The more we practice, the easier it becomes. The scriptures you will read this week serve as a reminder to practice self-discipline daily.

Passage of Meditation: 1 Corinthians 9:24-27 MSG

You've all been to the stadium and seen the athletes race. Everyone runs; one wins. Run to win. All good athletes train hard. They do it for a gold medal that tarnishes and fades. You're after one that's gold eternally. I don't know about you, but I'm running hard for the finish line. I'm giving it everything I've got. No sloppy living for me! I'm staying alert and in top condition. I'm not going to get caught napping, telling everyone else all about it and then missing out myself.

Prayer

Dear heavenly Father, thank you for the freedom of choice. Help me to make the right decisions and not conform to ways of the world. Give me strength as I train myself daily to have self-control, recognizing that the enemy will continue to tempt me as I grow in you.

Reflections

Take some time to reflect on this week's focus. Keep a journal for any thoughts, questions, and concerns that may arise while reading. You should also take some time to reflect and journal after each day's reading. You may want to journal prayer requests that come to mind after your reading this week's lesson.

DIVA Challenge #2

Record each time you were tempted to do something wrong, yet resisted. Explain the benefit from not giving in to temptation.

Day 1

"Do not waste time arguing over godless ideas and old wives' tales. Instead, train yourself to be godly." 1 Timothy 4:7

We often find ourselves caught up in the concerns of the world. We listen to and read the latest celebrity new. We discuss the latest gossip floating around our schools and jobs and we spend hours on social media commenting on who did what with whom and when. All of these activities are a waste of time and go against what God has called us to do.

Instead of reading the breaking news on TMZ, read your bible. Stop spreading rumors; instead spread the Gospel. Don't negatively comment on someone's social media post; comment on how good God has been to you. Stop spending your valuable time on useless activities. Having knowledge of worldly things will not bring you any closer to the eternal life that we seek. Train yourself to be more like God. It is a better use of your time and resources.

Reflect on your interactions with your peers. How much time do you spend discussing things not of God? How can you shift the focus of your conversations to reflect a godly life?

Notes of Reflection

_____

_____

_____

_____

_____

_____

_____

_____

Day 2

"A person without self-control is like a city with broken down walls." Proverbs 25:28

What would happen to a city if everyone acted on impulse? What would the world would be like if people said the first thing that came to their mind or if they did things without fear of the consequences? Though this idea is not far from the reality we live in, there are many people in the world who consciously try to do the right thing. They consider the consequences of their actions before they act. They also consider how their actions will affect others.

If everyone in the world lacked self-control, society would be destroyed. A lack of self-control is like an open invitation for Satan to take over your life. He is similar to the Trojan horse of Greek mythology; once he has taken your mind it is much easier for him to win. It is our job to stay in the word daily to protect ourselves from his attacks. We must use God's word as the walls of our fortress to block evil from taking over our lives.

Reflect on the last time you failed to exhibit self-control; what was the outcome of the situation? How much destruction did it cause? What would you still have today if it had not been for that decision?

Notes of Reflection

_____

_____

_____

_____

_____

_____

Day 3

"I discipline my body like an athlete, training it to do what it should. Otherwise, I fear that after preaching to others I myself might be disqualified." 1Corithians 9:27

Elite athletes train hard regularly to keep themselves in shape and to ensure they will perform at a high level. If they fail to train, they are likely to lose their ability to do well at their sport. This may cause them to loose favor with their coach or worse yet, be removed from the team. The kingdom of God is like a team and you are the elite athlete. You must constantly train your body to do the will of God so you can walk the Christian walk with authority.

When you fail to train, it is more difficult for you to resist the temptations of the devil. How are you going to be prepared for the spiritual war if you have not trained? When you train, through study of the bible, prayer, worship and gaining understanding is what allows us to use God's power to defeat Satan.

Reflect on a time when you caught someone contradicting themselves. How likely were you to trust this person again? Now consider if your action truly line up with your proclamations of your love for God. Are you a walking contradiction?

Notes of Reflection

_____

_____

_____

_____

_____

Day 4

"For God has not given us a spirit of fear and timidity, but of power, love and self-discipline." 2 Timothy 1:7

The world will have you convinced that practicing self-discipline is a difficult task. Satan will try to entice you with the easy way of life that is not concerned with the will of God. Technically they are telling you the truth. Consciously practicing self-discipline is a difficult task if you try to do it on your own.

The good news is where we are weak, God is strong and through him all things are possible. It is our duty to tap into that power and use what he has already given us. When we ask him for help, he is willing and able to provide us with what we need. For us as humans, the difficult task becomes trusting in his word. Believing when it tell us that he will never leave us nor forsake us. We are better off when we truly believe that we can walk on his power.

Reflect on the last time you felt like you could not control yourself in a situation. Did you ask God for help, did you seek him in your decision making or did you lean on your own power?

Notes of Reflection

_____
_____
_____
_____
_____
_____
_____
_____

Day 5

"Keep putting into practice all learned and received from me-everything you heard from me and saw me doing. Then the God of peace will be with you." Philippians 4:9

When we learned to wash our hair, the instructions were: wash, rinse, and repeat. This is how you train to live a godly life. You are to read the word (wash), practice its teachings (rinse) and repeat this process daily. It is this constant repetition that makes living an upright life a habit instead of a task that we dread.

When you consciously practice the teachings in the bible, the Holy Spirit will take up residence in your heart to help you along the way. He will guide your every thought, and decision. He will give us peace. His peace assures us that he is always there. Regardless of how difficult things get we are never alone. When we do not rely on him and turn to our own understanding we fail.

Reflect on a habit you have. What is something you subconsciously do daily? How did this become a habit? What are ways you can apply these principles to make the study and practice of the word of God a habit in your life?

Notes of Reflection

_____
_____
_____
_____
_____
_____
_____
_____

Day 6

"Rather, he must enjoy having guests in his home, and he must love what is good. He must live wisely and be just. He must live a devout life." Titus 1:8

Some people find the bible to be ambiguous and difficult to understand. However if your read carefully it is very clear. The problem most people have is they see and understand what they want to. The bible clearly states you must live a disciplined life. How could you possibly misinterpret that?

Not only does the bible clearly tell you what you should do, it also gives you clear instructions on how to do it. If you want to live a disciplined life, it will require daily practice. We must be dedicated to being better disciples and carrying out the will of God. We must be diligent in our study because the harder we work towards being like Christ the harder Satan will try to stop us. He does not want us to succeed.

Reflect on a time you received specific instructions; did you follow all the instructions or just some? What was the outcome of that situation? Often, when we choose to follow parts of the bible life does not turn out the way we imagined.

Notes of Reflection

Week 3: Integrity in Your Heart

I must carry integrity in my heart, for it is my heart that the Lord judges!

Integrity is a word most people don't use until they're in their mid-twenties. However, integrity is something you can practice starting at a young age. Showing integrity means not blaming your sibling for eating all the cookies, after you finished the last one. Integrity of the heart is being sincere, doing things not for the sake of show, but instead, because you know it is the right thing to do.

Integrity of the heart allows you to do good deeds for the sake of another, regardless of how those actions will be received. As people often say "at least your heart was in the right place." God is not concerned if the world praises you for living an upright life. He is more concerned that you lived an upright life. The scriptures you will read this week make clear

God's position on integrity, understand that he sees what the world cannot see.

Passage of Meditation: 2 Corinthians 1:12-14 MSG

Now that the worst is over, we're pleased we can report that we've come out of this with conscience and faith intact, and can face the world—and even more importantly, face you with our heads held high. But it wasn't by any fancy footwork on our part. It was God who kept us focused on him, uncompromised. Don't try to read between the lines or look for hidden meanings in this letter. We're writing plain, unembellished truth, hoping that you'll now see the whole picture as well as you've seen some of the details. We want you to be as proud of us as we are of you when we stand together before our Master Jesus.

Prayer

Dear heavenly Father, though the world will only perceive my actions you know my heart. Help me to guard my heart from the temptations of the world; help me to keep it pure, operating with integrity in everything I do. Lord, thank you for holding me accountable for not just my actions but also my intent.

Reflections

Take some time to reflect on this week's focus. Keep a journal for any thoughts, questions, and concerns that may arise while reading. You should also take some time to reflect and journal after each day's reading. You may want to journal prayer requests that come to mind after your reading this week's lesson.

DIVA Challenge #3

Record each time you were dishonest this week.

_____

_____

_____

_____

_____

_____

_____

_____

_____

_____

_____

_____

_____

_____

_____

_____

_____

_____

_____

_____

_____

_____

_____

_____

_____

_____

_____

_____

_____

_____

_____

Day 1

"Pray for us, for our conscience is clear and we want to live honorably in everything we do." Hebrews 13:18

It can be difficult to live honorably in everything you do, especially if you think no one is watching. The problem with that idea is even if no one is around, God is always watching. You become more aware as you listen to that little voice inside of you which constantly telling you what you are doing is wrong. That voice, your conscious better known as the Holy Spirit, keeps you honorable in everything you do. Open your ears and your heart to listen to it.

One way to ensure you remain honorable in everything is to keep the lines of communication between you and God open at all times. You should seek his advice in every situation. Over time, your relationship becomes so strong that you will begin to recognize his voice and hear him as he guides you in the right direction.

Reflect on a time when you did something wrong, and it weighed heavy on your mind for a long time. This was your conscious trying to reconcile your actions. Consider that nagging voice the next time you are tempted to be dishonest.

Notes of Reflection

_____
_____
_____
_____
_____
_____
_____
_____

Day 2

"The Lord detests people with crooked hears, but he delights in those with integrity." Proverbs 11:20

You know when someone is being "fake" with you. There is something in your gut that tells you this person is not being authentic. Sometimes you are the only person who notices while everyone else is blinded by their charm and kind words. That is exactly how God feels when he watches us from heaven. He may be the only one who notices when you are not being sincere. Those around you may be deceived by your charm but God is not. He always knows if your heart is in the right place.

Your first thought is often your most honest thought. It is what your heart truly believes. Your first thought is what you would say or do before considering the consequences of your actions. This is what God see's even before you open your mouth or make a move. People often say "honesty is the best policy". I would take it a step further and say "honesty is God's policy".

Think of the last time you thought someone was not being honest with you. How did that make you feel? Keep that in your remembrance when tempted to be deceitful. Your conscious should be clear in everything you do.

Notes of Reflection

_____

_____

_____

_____

_____

_____

_____

Day 3

"Let God weigh me on the scales of justice, for he knows my integrity." Job 31:6

Ever noticed when someone blames you for something you know you did not do? You want to launch a full scale investigation just to clear your name. Conversely, when you are guilty you are quick to accept whatever is thrown at you, just to get it over with. With God there is no investigation needed. He knows you better than you know yourself. He knows everything you've ever done: the good, the bad and the ugly. Since he knows you so well, he is the only judge and jury you need to worry about.

His justice is the ultimate justice. The standards by which he judges you are more stringent than anything the world could come up with. If you keep his commands and live according to His standards, you should not be concerned about accusations made by the world. Regardless of the outcome, justice will be served, either here on earth or in heaven.

Consider the last time you got blamed for something you didn't do. What was your reaction? Did you get upset and demand a full investigation or did you move on with the comfort that God knows your heart and nothing other than that really matters.

Notes of Reflection

_____

_____

_____

_____

_____

Day 4

"With Christ as my witness, I speak with utter truthfulness. My conscience and the Holy Spirit confirm it." Romans 9:1

It doesn't matter how hard you try, not everyone will believe you all the time. There will be people who challenge you. They will attempt to discredit you. They will do everything in their power to prove you are lying, even if they are wrong. Don't be discouraged by these circumstances. Take comfort in knowing God has the final say. He knows if you are right or wrong. Even if you are wrongly persecuted on earth you will be rewarded in heaven.

Some people are not worth arguing with. Sometimes the situation is a test to see if you are truly committed to living according to God's commands. If the Holy Spirit can confirm you are telling the truth, then you can ignore everyone else. This doesn't mean that you can walk around and ignore people because your position is correct. It does however; mean that you do not have to be concerned about the possible outcome. Eventually, God will vindicate you.

Reflect on a time someone tried to prove you were lying even though you were not. At some point was the truth revealed?

Notes of Reflection

_____

_____

_____

_____

_____

_____

Day 5

"May the integrity and honesty prot4ect me for I put my hope in you." Psalm 25:21

Integrity and honesty are like identical twins, you can't have one without the other. If you are honest, then you must be morally upright. Without integrity you are being dishonest. As you walk through life, integrity and honesty are the best protection you have against false witnesses. When you live a life according to God's standards, people will find it difficult to make false accusations against you. When they try, others will find it difficult to believe them. Their accusations will contradict the way you live.

When you live with integrity, God will protect you from the things you cannot handle. He takes note of the way we live and even if we are persecuted in the world, we will be glorified in heaven. God always has our back, no matter the situation. Our only requirement is to trust that he will protect us.

We are in constant need of protection. There is a constant spiritual war taking place around us. If we are not careful to remain honest and morally upright, we could end up on the wrong side of the battle. Consider your actions during difficult times. Do you remain honest and morally upright?

Notes of Reflection

_____
_____
_____
_____
_____
_____
_____

Day 6

"God blesses those who hearts are pure, for they will see God," Matthew 5:8

Would you surround yourself with people who you knew were up to no good? Would you intentionally keep the company of liars? If you wouldn't want to be around a person who was always trying to get over on you, why would you think God does? Our ability to enter the kingdom of heaven is dependent upon our hearts. What does your heart say about you?

If your heart is pure in everything you do and you keep his commands, judgement day will be more like a welcome home party. When you are deceitful, conniving and scheme to get your way, judgement day will God's bon voyage party for you. The good news is there is still time to get things right. As long as you have breath in your body, you can get right with God. You should work each day to keep your conscience clear.

Take inventory of your heart. What is your motivation? Are you living a godly life because you want to please God or are you living this life because of what you hope to gain? If your intent is not pure, your reward will not be what you expect.

Notes of Reflection

_____
_____
_____
_____
_____
_____
_____
_____

Week 4
Integrity in
Actions

I am a woman of my word, doing what is right in the eyes of God!

Integrity of actions is the one thing that is most difficult to hide. Even the world can see your actions. Most people can easily decipher if you are acting with integrity or not. Not following through on commitments puts your integrity into question. People begin to wonder if they can rely on you. For most people, it is most desirable to correct the undesirable qualities that people can see. Unfortunately this does not translate into people keeping their promises.

The reason people "flake" on their commitments stems from last week's lesson; their heart is not in the right place. It is better for you to decline than to default. By defaulting, you have sinned twice. First you lied (acted without a sincere heart) and then you didn't stay true to your word (acted without integrity).

Often we try to justify our actions, saying it wasn't that big of a deal or it was just a little white lie. However, such actions now comprise your ability to receive greater blessings. Think about it, if I can't trust you to take care of a goldfish why would I give you a dog? Likewise the bible says in Luke 16:10 "… if you are dishonest in little things, you won't be honest with greater responsibilities." Why compromise your destiny just to get out of something?

Passage of Meditation: Nehemiah 5:14-16 MSG

From the time King Artaxerxes appointed me as their governor in the land of Judah — from the twentieth to the thirty-second year of his reign, twelve years — neither I nor my brothers used the governor's food allowance. Governors who had preceded me had oppressed the people by taxing them forty shekels of silver (about a pound) a day for food and wine while their underlings bullied the people unmercifully. But out of fear of God I did none of that. I had work to do; I worked on this wall. All my men were on the job to do the work. We didn't have time to line our own pockets.

Prayer

Dear heavenly Father, guide my steps so they align with the love of you that is in my heart. Help me to act with integrity, to be honest in everything. Help me to show love and care in all I do. Help me to resist the temptation to take the easy way out. Instead help me to stay on the path you have laid out for me.

Reflections

Take some time to reflect on this week's focus. Keep a journal for any thoughts, questions, and concerns that may arise while reading. You should also take some time to reflect and journal after each day's reading. You may want to journal

prayer requests that come to mind after your reading this week's lesson.

DIVA Challenge #4

Apologize to each person that you were dishonest with from the previous week

_____
_____
_____
_____
_____
_____
_____
_____
_____
_____
_____
_____
_____
_____
_____
_____
_____
_____
_____
_____
_____
_____
_____
_____
_____
_____
_____
_____

Day 1

"Do to others as you would like them to do to you."
Luke 6:31

The golden rule is the first thing you learn about interacting with other people. If you don't want to be cheated, don't cheat. If you don't want to be lied to, don't lie. If you don't want to be disrespected, then be respectful. What the golden rule doesn't mean is do unto others as they do to you. This scripture is often misquoted. This leads people to believe they only have to be kind to those who are kind to them. However, God's requirement for your behavior is not contingent on the actions of others.

When you stand for judgement, God won't ask you if someone deserves the poor treatment you gave them. He will ask you if you kept his command. We are to be loving and kind regardless of the treatment we receive in return. We are to put out into the world the same consideration we seek from God. If God treated us the same way we treat him, most of us would feel used, abused and ignored.

Reflect on how you treat those around you. Consider how you feel when you are wronged. If you would be hurt by your own actions, then you are breaking the golden rule.

Notes of Reflection

_____
_____
_____
_____
_____
_____
_____

Day 2

"Better to be poor and honest than to be dishonest and rich,"
Proverbs 28:6

Most people would argue it is better to have money by any means necessary than to be poor. The bible tells us that the opposite is true. Earthly possessions are not eternal; you can't take your fancy car, mini mansion or designer shoes with you to heaven. It doesn't matter what you are wearing when they put you in the casket. Once you get to heaven everyone is wearing the same outfit. Everything you purchase will eventually end up in the trash, or in someone else's closet.

The poor honest man will live richly in eternity. What he earned is worth at least ten times more than all the dishonest wealthy man's possessions. No one can purchase eternal life, not even the richest man in the world. It's not for sale. This is not a condemnation of wealthy people, but a warning to those considering dishonest means to obtain wealth.

Reflect on you priorities. What matters most to you, living a life of integrity or gaining money? Consider what you stand to gain by choosing honesty over riches. You may find the need to re-prioritize things.

Notes of Reflection

_____
_____
_____
_____
_____
_____
_____
_____

Day 3

"The way of the Lord is a stronghold to those with integrity, but it destroys the wicked." Proverbs. 10:29

When you follow the commands of God, it is difficult not to behave with integrity. You will not be perfect. There will be times when you fall short. You will succumb to the temptations of the world. It is inevitable simply because we are human and we live in a fallen world. However, your integrity will draw you back to the ways of the Lord. You will repent, seek forgiveness and eventually your actions will align with the will of God.

The alternative for those without integrity is destruction. Even though you see deceitful people who seem to have everything, understand that the destruction is not always natural. God can destroy you without taking your earthly possessions. Instead losing your money, you may lose your mind, your relationships or even your health.

Has there ever been a time in your life when you feel defeated yet everyone around you seem to think you have it all together. Reflect on your recent actions; you may realize you have been lacking integrity.

Notes of Reflection

_____
_____
_____
_____
_____
_____
_____

Day 4

"If you are faithful in the little things, you will be faithful in the large ones. But if you are dishonest in the little things, you won't be honest with greater responsibilities." Luke 16:10

Past behavior is a good indicator of future behavior. God knows your heart. He knows if you're a being honest in all situations. If you are dishonest when the consequences are small, what motivation do you have to exhibit integrity when the stakes are high? If you believe you are getting away with lying you will continue to lie. The only way not to be condemned to hell is to turn from your dishonest ways.

God wants you to show integrity in the small tasks. He wants you to perform as if you are doing it directly for him. Once you have this concept mastered, it will be easier to maintain integrity when you are given great responsibility. Eventually, integrity becomes part of who you are. It becomes so ingrained in your heart that people and God will know they can trust you with any and everything.

Do you practice walking with integrity daily? Reflect on the areas of your life that could use improvement. What small tasks have you not been faithful with?

Notes of Reflection

_____
_____
_____
_____
_____
_____
_____

Day 5

"The godly walk with integrity; blessed are their children who follow them." Proverbs 20:7

As a believer your life is a walking billboard for God. When you proclaim to love the lord, your actions should reflect that. When they don't, you may cause others to question what it means to be a Christian. When your actions and words do not align, you are not only causing damnation unto yourself but also misleading those under your influence. If there is no difference between how you and the non-believer behaves, what is the point of becoming a believer?

When you diligently walk with integrity, others are more likely to follow your example. They will notice that there is something different about you. They will see how you stand out from the crowd. Your life may be the only example of Christian living they have and it could make or break their relationship with God. Do you want to be responsible for someone turning away from God?

If your life was a reality show, would it honor God or could it only air after hours on HBO? Just because your life isn't being recorded for TV, there is always someone watching.

Notes of Reflection

_____
_____
_____
_____
_____
_____
_____
_____

Day 6

"Work willingly at whatever you do, as though you were working for the Lord rather than for people." Colossians 3:23

Often we look at our daily tasks and think God doesn't care. He is not worried about if I give 100% of my energy to everything I do. We believe it is ok to slack off on certain tasks, the ones that seem unimportant. We approach them with disdain and do the bare minimum just to get by. This is not pleasing to God. He wants us to approach every task in life as if we are doing it specifically for him.

Remember he is always watching; he sees when we lack effort at school or work. He knows when we are taking advantage of our circumstances. However, we must remember that he has set a standard for the way we are to live. We must adhere to his standards regardless of the circumstances. When you live to please God in everything you do, even your most dreaded tasks are bearable.

What is God watching when he looks at your life? Reflect on how you approach the things you dread doing. Do you hurry through tasks? Do you do the bare minimum just to get by or do your give it 100 percent as if you are doing it for God?

Notes of Reflection

_____
_____
_____
_____
_____
_____
_____

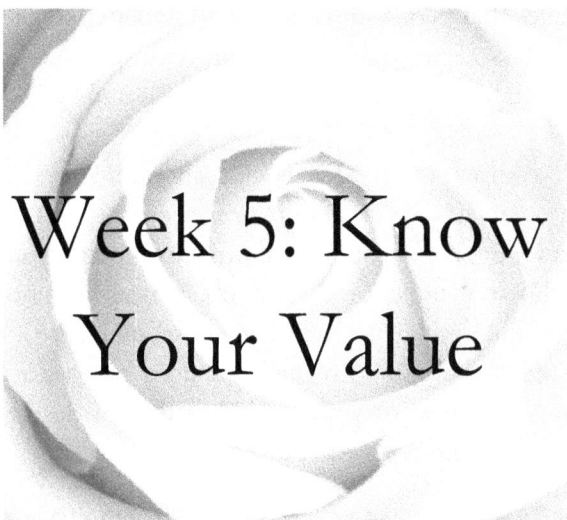

Week 5: Know Your Value

I know that I am worth more than gold. My body is a temple that belongs to God.

It's an often repeated sentiment to young women, "you are worth more than gold" or "your body is a temple"; but there is a reason for that. Think about how valued gold is in our society. Think about how much people pay for things made of pure gold. This is not a suggestion to sell your self. It is a suggestion to think about how little you require of people for your time, love and attention. Are you someone that a person has to sacrifice for or are you available to any and every one with no set expectations?

A temple is a sacred place that not everyone can enter. You must meet specific criteria to gain access and if you break a rule, your access can be revoked. What are the specific requirements you have for people to gain access to you? What are the rules that people must follow to remain part of your life? Do you disassociate from people who violate those boundaries you have established? Have you ever established boundaries?

To know your value is not about being stuck up or isolating yourself. It is about not accepting less than the promises God has for you. It is about surrounding yourself with people who see you as God sees you. It is about knowing you are worth the wait. You are worth the time, the effort, the respect and the praise. Anyone who does not see it that way should not be a part of your life. They do not deserve to reap the benefits of being part of your world.

Passage of Meditation; Luke 12:6-7

What's the price of two or three pet canaries? Some loose change, right? But God never overlooks a single one. And he pays even greater attention to you, down to the last detail – even numbering the hairs on your head! So don't be intimidated by all this bully talk. You're worth more than a million canaries.

Prayer

Dear heavenly Father, thank you for sacrificing your only son for me. Help me to live a life that honors the temple that is my body, which you carefully designed. Help me to walk away from the people and things who do not respect my value and place people in my life who will see me as you see me.

Reflections

Take some time to reflect on this week's focus. Keep a journal for any thoughts, questions, and concerns that may arise while reading. You should also take some time to reflect and journal after each day's reading. You may want to journal

prayer requests that come to mind after your reading this week's lesson.

DIVA Challenge #5

Every day for the next week write one positive insight about yourself.

_____
_____
_____
_____
_____
_____
_____
_____
_____
_____
_____
_____
_____
_____
_____
_____
_____
_____
_____
_____
_____
_____
_____
_____
_____
_____
_____
_____
_____
_____
_____

Day 1

"So do not be afraid; you are more valuable to God than a whole flock of sparrows." Matthew 10:31

Every girl has that one pair of shoes she absolutely adores. The pair you only bring out on special occasions. When you take them off, you place them back inside the box wrapped in tissue paper. You treat these shoes as if they are the most important thing in the world to you. To God, you are more valuable than those shoes. To God, you are worth more than anything in the world.

You are his greatest creation and nothing concerns him more than your well-being. He knows, every hurt and every moment of joy in your life. He knows everything right down to the number of hairs on your head. You wouldn't let your favorite pair of shoes be destroyed. God's protection is even greater. He never leaves our side. You have round-the-clock security, just like an heir to a great kingdom should.

Reflect on your daily walk. Is it indicative of an heir to the throne or does your life reflect that of a fearful pauper? God values you too much for you not to value yourself.

Notes of Reflection

_____

_____

_____

_____

_____

_____

_____

_____

Day 2

"God saved you by his grace when you believed. And you can't take credit for this; it is a gift from God." Ephesians 8:28

You would take exception if someone tried to take credit for your work. You may not say anything, but you would take a mental note. This is exactly how God feels when we try to take credit for the good things in our life. When we walk around with our heads held high as if we did all the heavy lifting. He is not pleased when we behave as if our accomplishments are due to our own abilities. Remember, Jesus shed his blood on the cross for our sins; that's a huge investment.

God's grace keeps you daily. He is constantly investing his time and power into your life. He does it because you are worth it. Everything you have, you owe to him. He gives to us freely because we are his children. We were made in his likeness. All he requires is acknowledgement and praise for what he has done. Stop taking credit for his hard work and give honor where honor is due.

Think about the blessings in your life. Do you give credit where credit is due or do you claim the praise for yourself? God didn't invest in your life so you could take his name out of the credits.

Notes of Reflection

_____

_____

_____

_____

_____

_____

Day 3

"For you know that God paid a ransom to save you from the empty life you inherited from your ancestors. And it was not paid with mere Gold or silver which lose their value."
1 Peter 1:18

In most kidnapping movies the story line goes something like this: the women is taken and then an obscenely large amount of money is demanded. Her family pays, and the women is returned to her old life. For the believer, the outcome is much better. Instead of money or things that depreciate, God gave his only son to pay our ransom. The value was so great, we don't have to return to our old life.

When we accept Christ as our personal savior and realize exactly how much he gave up for us, we can see that our new life has so much potential. We have the opportunity to live in paradise for eternity. The cost of sin is far too expensive to pay on your own. Without the sacrifice of Christ we would still be held captive by our sins.

Is the life you live worth the ransom God has paid? Reflect on how you carry yourself. Do you dress provocatively, use profanity, lie, cheat or steal? Do you present yourself according to your heavenly value?

Notes of Reflection

_____
_____
_____
_____
_____
_____
_____

Day 4

"Run from sexual sin! No other sin so clearly affects the body as this one does. For sexual immorality is a sin against your own body." 1 Corinthians 6:18

In horror movies, while everyone else is running, there is usually that one person who stands and looks around. Why is that? Do they not realize something detrimental is about to happen? Are they trying to test the villain and see if he will actually come after them? Unfortunately, this is how we have become with sexual immorality. God tells us to run from it; but instead we get close. We dip our toes in to "test" the water thinking we are in complete control.

Society has tried to convince us that there is nothing wrong with sex outside of marriage. The problem is, his rationale goes against the word of God. Most other sins are committed outside of the body. They do not directly affect the same place we ask God to dwell in. Sexual relations is a benefit reserved for the relationship God ordains for you; marriage.

Consider your relationships with men. Are you running from sexual immorality or are you dipping you toe in to test the temperature? The longer you stay around temptation, the more likely you are to succumb to it.

Notes of Reflection

_____

_____

_____

_____

_____

_____

_____

Day 5

"For God bought you with a high price. So you must honor God with your body." 1 Corinthians 6:20

Your body is not community property. It was not designed to be viewed by all. It was not designed to be used, abused and returned damaged and broken. Think about the complexity of the human body. How integrated each part is with the other. God took his time to create us; he carefully assigned each part a function. Something so well crafted is of great value. It should be admired for its beauty and design not bought, sold and traded for things that lose value.

Honoring God with your body means preserving it to be used for His purpose and to His glory. Take care of yourself so you have the health and strength to carry out your divine purpose. You should watch what you eat and exercise regularly. Be sure to stay away from drugs, alcohol and anything else that may damage the body. We must refrain from fornicating and other activities that may negatively affect our bodies. The condition of our bodies should match the high price God paid for us.

Does your life reflect the true value of your body? Do you care for yourself in a way that honors God? Consider if your Retail Price matches the Manufacture's Suggested Retail Price.

Notes of Reflection

_____
_____
_____
_____
_____

Day 6

"But God showed his great love for us by sending Christ to die for us while we were still sinners." Romans 5:8

In this society, very few things are handed to you for free. You are required to work for and earn everything you have. This is especially true for relationships. Everyone expects something in return. We only love when loved. No one will spend time and energy sacrificing for you if you don't deserve it. Additionally, the size of your reward is directly correlated to your effort. The harder you work to be like Christ, the greater your reward will be.

Fortunately for us, that is not how God works. If it was, most of us would not receive his blessings. He saw the value in us long before we realized the error of our ways. He knows, despite our actions there is something in us worth saving. This is why Jesus was sacrificed on the cross; not in response to our deeds but in spite of them. How many people are you willing to do that for?

Based on what God has sacrificed for you, do you live in a way that honors his sacrifice? Was your salvation worth the life of Christ? Live in a way that honors the sacrifice God made on your behalf.

Notes of Reflection

_____

_____

_____

_____

_____

_____

Week 6: Value Others

I will value others; showing them the love of the Lord!

We often think of valuing others as a direct interaction between two people. But what about gossip, deliberate exclusion from a group or activity, not speaking to the person who just walked into a room and failing to acknowledge someone's presence? These are all examples of not valuing another person. A smile can show a person you see them as a human who deserves kindness. God places a high value on all of his creations. No one life is worth more than another. No one person's feelings carry more significance than someone else's.

You have probably heard the phrase "sticks and stones can break my bones but words could never hurt me". However, the bible says "The tongue can bring death or life" (Prov. 18:21). Your words have power; they have the power to lift someone up or tear someone down. They have the power to create great opportunity and to give praise and honor to others. Your words also have the ability to destroy someone. Use the power of your words for good.

Everyone does not have to be your friend. Everyone will not like you. This does not make them less valuable as a person. They may not have a purpose in your life. Their purpose in your life may be to challenge you, to push into a new level of success. You may not always like them. You may never like them. That is the great thing about the word of God, it does not require you to like anyone. It does however, require you to love everyone. Love is showing respect for people just because they are a person.

Passage of Meditation: John 13: 34-35 MSG

Let me give you a new command: Love one another. In the same way I loved you, you love one another. This is how everyone will recognize that you are my disciples – when they see the love you have fir each other.

Prayer

Dear heavenly Father, guide my steps so they align with the love of you that is in my heart. Help me to value others because they are people. Lord help me to refrain from words of destruction. Help me to use my words to uplift and praise others, practicing the golden rule daily.

Reflections

Take some time to reflect on this week's focus. Keep a journal for any thoughts, questions, and concerns that may arise while reading. You should also take some time to reflect and journal after each day's reading. You may want to journal

prayer requests that come to mind after your reading this week's lesson.

DIVA Challenge #6

Every day for the next week give at least one person a compliment about them as a person, record their name and the compliment that you paid them.

_____
_____
_____
_____
_____
_____
_____
_____
_____
_____
_____
_____
_____
_____
_____
_____
_____
_____
_____
_____
_____
_____
_____
_____

Day 1

"Now may the LORD value my life, even as I have valued yours today. May he rescue me from all my troubles," 1 Samuel 26:24

Have you ever been nice just for the sake of being nice? In today's society our actions and interactions have become about "what I can gain from the situation". Rarely do we think about what others gain from our actions or encounters. However this is exactly how God wants us to behave. He wants us to consider the needs of others over ourselves. He wants us to value others just as much or even more than we do ourselves.

When we value others, we are setting ourselves up for greater blessings. Our reward in heaven is directly tied to how we treat people on earth. When we value others, the Lord is pleased with us. We are fulfilling his number one command; to love our neighbors as ourselves. When we take people for granted, mistreat or ignore them we are jeopardizing our favor with God.

Consider how you interact with people. Not just those you know and see regularly but strangers as well. Do you value them the way God instructs us to? Remember the golden rule, it applies to all situations.

Notes of Reflection

Day 2

"Instead, be kind to each other, tenderhearted, forgiving one another, just as God through Christ has forgiven you."
Ephesians 4:32

We are all hypocrites! Yes, it is harsh and you are probably saying to yourself "I'm not a hypocrite" but you are. Every time someone wrongs you and you hold it against them, you are being a hypocrite. If God treated us that way, no one would go to heaven. We would all be doomed to an eternity in hell without his mercy.

What right do we have not to be kind, loving, caring and forgiving? This is the way God treats us every single day. He doesn't check our record before he decides to love us. Whatever is valuable to God should be valuable to us. We should treat people the same way we expect God to treat us. You cannot pick and choose who to love. There are no exceptions.

Do you value what God values? Are you being kind, loving and forgiving of others? Consider what life would be like if God treated you the way you treat others. It may be time to turn over a new leaf.

Notes of Reflection

_____

_____

_____

_____

_____

_____

_____

Day 3

"Love each other with genuine affection and take delight in honoring each other." Romans 12:10

Some people really enjoy being the center of attention. They thrive off of being honored and adored. They are the popular kids in school. The people everyone wants to be friends with. The popular kids however, do not always share the praise. Some people find it difficult to celebrate others. They have a hard time not being the center of attention.

God want us to love each other so much that we are excited to celebrate each other. He wants us to be able to cheer each other on without a hidden agenda. Not an artificial praise, one you give out of obligation. He wants us to be genuinely excited for the triumphs of others and celebrate them as if we were celebrating ourselves. Learn to view others success as a sign of inspiration.

Reflect on a moment when someone was honored instead of you. Did you harbor ill feelings or were you able to bask in their glory with them? Can you celebrate their accomplishments without thinking about yourself?

Notes of Reflection

_____

_____

_____

_____

_____

_____

_____

_____

Day 4

"This is my commandment: Love each other in the same way I have loved you,". John 15:12

God's love for us is unconditional. There are no prerequisites, no qualifications or contingencies. The only people on earth who will ever come close to loving you that way is your parents, otherwise the love of another human has conditions. We love our friends but only if they behave a certain way, we love our family as long as they don't hurt us. Most of us don't love strangers, but we are generally kind to them as long as they are not bothering us.

You see there are lots of conditions for other to receive love and affection from us. Now imagine what life would be like if God's love for us came with the same conditions. Somehow he manages to look past out actions, the hurt we cause him when we don't obey his commands and our constant nagging and begging.

Reflect on you relationships with the people in your life. What are the conditions under which you show them love and affections? What can you do differently to love everyone unconditionally? Strive to love everyone the same way all the time regardless if they deserve it or not.

Notes of Reflection

_____

_____

_____

_____

_____

_____

Day 5

"Respect everyone and love the family of believers. Fear God and respect the king." 1 Peter 2:17

Sometimes the most difficult people to love is other Christians. The bible commands us to respect everyone, but it specifically calls on us to love other Christians. This includes the woman in church who talked about you for wearing a short skirt last week and the man in parking lot who cut you off so he could get the good spot.

The hurt caused by "church folk" often cuts the deepest and takes the longest to heal. This is because we tend to place other Christians on a pedestal. We expect them to behave a certain way and refrain from saying certain things. Once we understand that we are all flawed and accept that we all make mistake, we will be better able to move past those hurts. We are all a work in progress.

Reflect on a time you were hurt or offended by another Christian. Did this change you attitude towards God? Did it change the way you treated that person? The next time you are hurt by another believer remember that we are all a work in progress and love them anyway.

Notes of Reflection

_____

_____

_____

_____

_____

_____

_____

_____

Day 6

"Beware that you don't look down on any of these little ones.
For I tell you that in heaven their angels are always in the
presence of my heavenly Father." Matthew 18:10

It is human nature for us to compare ourselves to others. We look at people and think they must have more/less than I do. This type of thinking contradicts how God want us to behave. He wants us to think of each other equally. No one person should be treated better than another. Jesus didn't come to the earth for the rich, famous and privileged. In fact, he was often at odds with those who held the most power, the wealthy and the rulers of the land. He came to serve the common people; those in need and the ones exiled by the community.

If Jesus served those who were the least important, we should do the same. We are not above or too good to associate with social outcasts. These are the people we should run to. Pleasing God is about how you treated those who could do nothing for you in return.

Consider your motives and thoughts the next time you encounter someone that the world sees as less valuable. Think of their angels as God's most trusted advisors. What report would they give on you?

Notes of Reflection

_____
_____
_____
_____
_____
_____
_____

Week 7: Selfish Ambition

I will not be boastful or give in to the selfish ambitions of the world!

Ambition is generally a good quality to have. Where you get into trouble is when your motives are not pure (integrity of heart) or you use deceitful practices to get what you want (integrity in actions). The bible calls this selfish ambition, where your sole focus is self, you operate without regard to any other party involved. As long as you get what you want, everything is ok. This may get you the money, the fame and the "friends" that you seek. What it won't get you is a place in heaven.

God wants you to be ambitions; he wants you to strive to be better. He wants you to have the desires of your heart. He wants you to live a fruitful and prosperous life. He also wants you to walk the path he laid out for you; he knows where it leads. He knows all the awesome things he has in store for you.

Most people get caught up in selfish ambition is because they take their focus away from God. They become obsessed with the world's definition of wealth and success.

Instead of striving for more money or fame, strive to live the life God designed for you. It may require more work. It may not be what you expected and it may not fit the world's view of what you should do. However, if you stay focused on God and not on the world you will live a life that is far greater that you could have ever imagined.

Passage of Meditations Galatians 5: 19-21 MSG

It is obvious what kind of life develops out of trying to get your own way all the time: repetitive, loveless, cheap sex; a stinking accumulation of mental and emotional garbage; frenzied and joyless grabs for happiness; trinket gods; magic-show religion; paranoid loneliness; cutthroat competition; all-consuming-yet-never-satisfied wants; a brutal temper; an impotence to love or be loved; divided homes and divided lives; small-minded and lopsided pursuits; the vicious habit of depersonalizing everyone into a rival; uncontrolled and uncontrollable addictions; ugly parodies of community. I could go on. This isn't the first time I have warned you, you know. If you use your freedom this way, you will not inherit God's kingdom.

Prayer

Dear heavenly Father, help me to remain humble in all I do. Help me to live a life pleasing in your sight. Help me to not compromise my values to receive praise from the world. I pray that through my work people see you.

Reflections

Take some time to reflect on this week's focus. Keep a journal for any thoughts, questions, and concerns that may arise while reading. You should also take some time to reflect and journal after each day's reading. You may want to journal prayer requests that come to mind after your reading this week's lesson.

DIVA Challenge #7

Write down what profession you would like to have as an adult. Describe how you can use that profession to help others.

_____

_____

_____

_____

_____

_____

_____

_____

_____

_____

_____

_____

_____

_____

_____

_____

_____

_____

_____

_____

Day 1

"Those others do not have pure motives as they preach about Christ. They preach with selfish ambition, not sincerely, intending to make my chains more painful to me." 1 Thessalonians 4:11

Humans are selfish. There is no other way to put it; we were born this way. Everything that we do is in some way connected to the benefit we will receive. This includes our decision to follow Christ. Our initial decision is often driven by why the relationship can do for us. Our motives are not always sincere nor are we consistent in our discipleship. How does he feel when we say we serve him but only when it is convenient or beneficial to us? How would you feel?

The fastest way to destruction is to step all over people or being dishonest as you climb the ladder of success. Whatever you achieve with motives that are not pure will not last. Eventually, you will reap what you have sown. It may not happen on earth, but God has the final say.

Reflect on your life; think about what you say and how you live. Do they align or is there a conflict? When our words do not match our actions it is often because we are trying to be deceitful. Make sure your words and actions on the same page.

Notes of Reflection

_____
_____
_____
_____
_____
_____
_____

Day 2

"And what do you benefit if you gain the whole world but are yourself lost or destroyed?" Luke 9:25

You have probably heard the saying "you sold your soul to the devil". While you may not have literally made a transaction with Satan, operating with motives that are not pure, using people to get ahead, lying and cheating are basically the same thing. All the aforementioned behaviors are pleasing to Satan, not God. God wants you to follow his commands even if that means you will make less money, live in a smaller house and don't have a new car. He wants you do live according to His will, even when it is not the popular choice.

Satan delights when you do the things that God despises. As long as you live to the glory of Satan it draws you further away from God. You relationship with him becomes strained and you begin to lose sight of what really matters in life. You become consumed with material and social gains instead of fulfilling your divine purpose.

Consider how you approach life and your desire to be successful. Is your method "by any means necessary" or do you strive to do what is right even if that leads to less gain?

Notes of Reflection

_____

_____

_____

_____

_____

_____

_____

_____

Day 3

"You want what you don't have, so you scheme and kill to get
it. You are jealous of what others have, but you can't get it, so
you fight and wage war to take it away from them. Yet you
don't have what you want because you don't ask God for it."
James 4:2

Jealousy and envy are common in our society. We look
at what other people have and imagine how our lives would be
if we had those things. Many times we find it difficult to be
happy for people. We are unable to celebrate their
accomplishments because of our jealousy. We are unable to see
past our selfish desires to celebrate their blessings. Our desire to
be the best causes us to be envious.

We find reasons to downplay someone's success when
we feel it surpasses our own. We become so concerned with
what we don't have, we fail to appreciate what we do have. Yet
we don't have either because we didn't ask, or we didn't work
for it. Most times we don't even want what others have.

Think about the last time you were jealous or envious of
someone else. What made you feel this way? Did you prayerfully
ask God for those things? Did you put in the hard work and
dedication necessary to obtain those things?

Notes of Reflection

_____

_____

_____

_____

_____

_____

Day 4

"The godliness of good people rescues them; the ambition of treacherous people traps them." Proverbs 11:6

How many times have you tried to accomplish something but got stuck in the same place regardless of how hard you try? What is it that is keeping you from moving to the next step? What is keeping you from succeeding? Sometimes God will block us from heading to far down the wrong path. Other times it is our motives keeping us from succeeding. If we have self-serving motives for embarking on a particular journey we are likely operating outside of God's will.

If this is the case, we may find it difficult to succeed. We may find that we face more obstacles and setbacks than others who we know have journeyed down the same path. Instead of finding the answers to our questions we are left with more questions. When we allow our own goals and to take the place of God's will, we subject ourselves to unnecessary hardships.

Reflect on a goal that you tried to accomplish and faced considerable hardships or setbacks. What were your motives? Evaluate why you want to pursue something in life and be sure your goals align with God's will for your life.

Notes of Reflection

_____

_____

_____

_____

_____

_____

_____

_____

Day 5

"For wherever there is jealousy and selfish ambition, there you will find disorder and evil of every kind,". James 3:16

Have you ever been part of a group where everyone wanted to be the leader? In these situations, very little is accomplished and there is usually chaos and disorder. Everyone is more concerned about getting their way than accomplishing the goal. These types of groups usually don't last very long or the outcome is disastrous. The common goal is pushed to the side in the interest of individual goals.

This is what happens in life when there is selfishness and jealousy. You find yourself fighting against God and his will for your life. However, unlike fighting against other people fighting against God is futile. You will never win. Eventually, you will either surrender to his will or you will do as you please and surrender your relationship with God. Either way you lose. A life separate from God is not a life worth living.

Are you always seeking to get your own way instead of doing what is best for the greater good? The next time you find yourself faced with chaos and strife, consider what the end goal is. Are you working for self or are you working for others?

Notes of Reflection

_____
_____
_____
_____
_____
_____
_____
_____

Day 6

"Don't be selfish; don't try to impress others. Be humble, thinking of others as better than yourselves." Philippians 2:3

In this age of social media, so much of what we do aims to impress others. We post pictures of the good food we eat, the fun places we visit and the nice things we have. Rarely do we give credit where credit is due. We fail to acknowledge God as the source of all we have. We give the impression that we somehow accomplished these things on our own.

Self-importance causes us to look down on those who may have less than we do. It makes us believe that we are better because we are in a better financial situation. The reality is your bank account has no bearing on your heavenly position. God wants us to humble ourselves, acknowledge that he is the source of all that we have and hold others above ourselves. He wants us to use what we have for the uplifting of his kingdom.

Before you post another status update or picture on social media consider your reasoning. Are you doing it just to be seen? Be sure what you put out into the world is to the benefit of the kingdom and not the benefit of self.

Notes of Reflection

_____
_____
_____
_____
_____
_____
_____
_____
_____

Week 8: Godly Ambition

I work to keep my actions aligned with God's will!

Godly ambition is the desire to do what he designed you to do. To use the unique set of gifts and talents he gave you to give him glory. Notice I didn't say make money or support yourself. The reason is the bible is clear, God will supply ALL of your needs. All you have to do is follow him. Seek to do things the world deems as impossible. Let your life be a living testimony to "I can do all things through Christ that strengthens me" That is godly ambition!

You may be at a point in your life where you do not have a clear career path. You may not have figured out what God has called you to do. However, there is one thing you can be certain of, he does have a plan for you.

God wants us to have an abundant life. But what is God's definition of abundant? Is everyone supposed to be a millionaire? The short answer is no. God did not call everyone to have Oprah Winfrey's media success, LeBron James's skill set or Jay-z's musical talents. Even if you have similar talents, your path may not lead you to the same level of fame and fortune. Focus on God's will for your life and everything else will fall into place.

Passage of meditation: Psalm 37:1-6

Don't bother your head with braggarts or wish you could succeed like the wicked. In no time they'll shrivel like grass clippings and wilt like cut flowers in the sun. Get insurance with God and do a good deed, settle down and stick to your last. Keep company with God, get in on the best. Open up before God, keep nothing back; he'll do whatever needs to be done: He'll validate your life in the clear light of day and stamp you with approval at high noon.

Prayer

Dear heavenly Father, thank you for the gifts and talents you have given me. I pray that I may use them to bring glory to you. Help me to go through life with godly ambition. Help me to stay focused on the plan you have designed for my life.

Reflections

Take some time to reflect on this week's focus. Keep a journal for any thoughts, questions, and concerns that may arise while reading. You should also take some time to reflect and journal after each day's reading. You may want to journal prayer requests that come to mind after your reading this week's lesson.

DIVA Challenge #8

Now consider you future profession and outline what you will need from God to achieve that goal. Ask yourself if that goal aligns with the gifts and talents God has given you.

_____

_____

_____

_____

_____

_____

_____

_____

_____

_____

_____

_____

_____

_____

_____

_____

_____

_____

_____

_____

_____

_____

_____

_____

_____

_____

_____

_____

Day 1

"God blesses those who are humble, for they will inherit the whole earth." Matthew 5:5

The dictionary defines humility as "a modest or low view of one's own importance". This is a recurring theme throughout the bible. Even Jesus the King was humble. He credited the success of his work to his heavenly Father. He knew that his ability to perform miracles was not due to his own strength. He could have decided to do his own thing, especially when times were difficult. Yet he surrendered himself to the will of God; even when it called for him to be nailed to the cross.

However, his reward was to sit at the right hand of God. When we humble ourselves to God's will, we are working towards a similar reward. We are working towards eternal life with him. On the other hand when we look at ourselves as the most important piece of the puzzle, we are jeopardizing that reward.

As you work either inside the church or out in the world consider the reward you are working for. If you begin to think that you are more important thank the work; you should ask God to help realign your goals with his.

Notes of Reflection

_____
_____
_____
_____
_____
_____
_____

Day 2

"For I know the plans I have for you," says the LORD. "They are plans for good and not for disaster, to give you a future and a hope,". Jeremiah 29:11

Our best opportunity to succeed in life is to follow the plans God has made for us. Before we were conceived, he mapped out our life. He determined our starting point and our end point. He gives us a purpose to fulfill on this earth. He also gave us the freedom of choice; we can choose to follow him or we can choose not to.

Unfortunately, we live in a fallen world, full of temptations and opportunities for us to deviate from God's plan. We choose to ignore that he is our creator. As such he knows exactly what is best for us. He also knows exactly what we are destined to be. If we believe that he loves us and if we believe that he wants what is best for us, why do we choose to ignore what he tells us to do?

Before you make a decision or go too far down a particular path consult with God. Ask him if this is part of his plan for your life. If you take the time to develop a relationship with him he will guide you and he will lead you to where he wants you to go.

Notes of Reflection

_____

_____

_____

_____

_____

_____

Day 3

"Each time he said, *My grace is all you need. My power works best in weakness.* So now I am glad to boast about my weaknesses, so that the power of Christ can work through me."
2 Corinthians 12:9

He is the alpha and the omega, the beginning and the end. He is all powerful and all things are possible through him. These are phrases you have probably heard; but what do they mean? These scriptures are trying to illustrate the power of God. We as humans are limited. We have a finite amount of power, ability and strength. Our life span is finite, regardless of how old we grow to be. Eventually, we will die.

What these quotes are telling us is that God is not limited. He has all the power, strength and ability. He is eternal; he was before we were born and he will be after we die. If you have access to something that great, why would you rely on your own abilities? As believers we should be glad that we are limited. The more limited we are the more God can show us and the world how unlimited he is.

Consider how you plan out the next steps in your life. Do you make your decisions based on your own ability or do you consider the abilities of God.

Notes of Reflection

_____

_____

_____

_____

_____

_____

_____

Day 4

"And we know that God causes everything to work together for the good of those who love God and are called according to his purpose for them." Romans 8:28

Do you know what God has placed you on this earth to accomplish? When most people read Romans 8:28, they tend to leave out the last part of the verse, "and are called according to his purpose for them". This is the most important part of the verse. We cannot expect everything to work together for our good if we are not operating in the will of God. In fact, when we are operating outside of his purpose, we can expect greater hardships, more setbacks, and more failures.

Taking our own path and leaning to our own understanding does not set us up for greater blessings. In the end they lead us down a path of destruction. On the other hand, when we answer the call on our life, and work towards fulfilling his purpose for our lives, we can expect everything to work out in our favor.

Consider some difficult times that you have faced in your life. Did things work out in the end or did they go from bad to worse? What lead you to that situation? Were you walking in the will of God or had you decided to follow your own desires?

Notes of Reflection

_____

_____

_____

_____

_____

_____

Day 5

"Tainted wealth has no lasting value but right living can save your life." Proverbs 10:2

Tainted wealth, dirty money, easy money, fast money, you can call it whatever you want. If it was obtained through methods which are not pleasing to God, it has no value in the kingdom of God. It doesn't matter if it is money, social status, career achievements or relationships. If you want to have eternal life in heaven you must live an upright life. You may not see the fruits of you labor in this lifetime, but you will reap the rewards in eternity.

Heaven isn't a social club that you can buy your way into. You are not placed at the top of the list just because you have reached a certain status or position. You have to earn your way into heaven by living the way God wants you to live. God's standard of living does not include obtaining wealth, status, and power the easy way. Anything worth keeping, anything that will stand the test of time requires hard work, dedication, and patience.

If we want to receive the ultimate reward we must stay focused on the will of God. Evaluate your methods and your motives and make sure they are in line with God's standard of living.

Notes of Reflection

_____

_____

_____

_____

_____

_____

Day 6

"Seek the Kingdom of God above all else, and live righteously, and he will give you everything you need."   Matthew 6:33

We go to school to get and education so we can get a good job to provide for ourselves and our future families. This is how we are able to obtain the necessities in life; food, clothing and shelter. If we work hard enough we may even be able to obtain some of our wants as well. Sometimes we will lie, cheat and steal to get to the top. We overwork ourselves to obtain the things of this world, to look good in the eyes of others.

God has not called us to chase the things of this world. We are called to seek his kingdom, to do the things that glorify him. To live in a way that fulfills his purpose and uplifts his people. We should strive to be more and more like him daily. When we follow his instructions, we will have everything that we need. When we are truly focused on the will of God our wants become his wants.

Reflect on the reasons you do the things that you do. Are you working for an earthly purpose or are you working for a godly purpose? Check you motives to be sure they align with His will.

Notes of Reflection

_____
_____
_____
_____
_____
_____
_____
_____

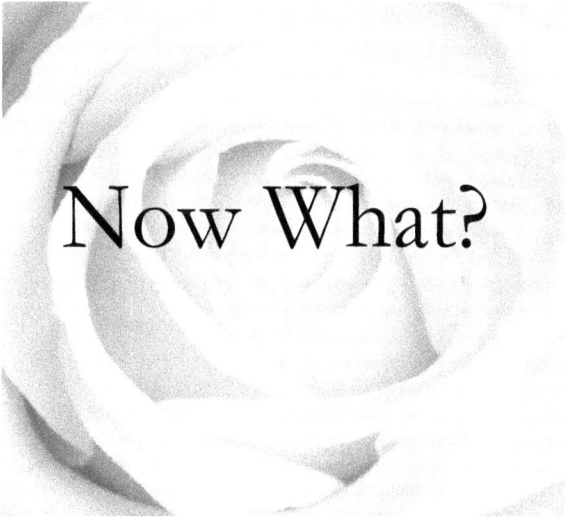

Now What?

Now that you have completed this journey, you are probably wondering what's next. Allow your light to shine so bright people will wonder what is so different about you? Be disciplined in everything you do. Work diligently towards your goals and don't allow others to distract you from what you know you have to do. Know when to accept correction from you elders, remember that they do it out of love and not malice. It is their duty as part of the village that nurtures you to help keep you on the right path. Take the opportunity to use those moments as valuable lessons on life. They will serve you well.

Show integrity; always be honest and upfront with people. Be a woman of your word and operate with sincere intentions. Do not be deceitful and tell lies; those things are not becoming of a godly woman. They will not bring you favor in heaven or on earth. Understand people may not acknowledge the good you do, but do good anyway. The Lord sees your heart and will reward you accordingly.

Know your value and respect others who are equally valuable. Surround yourself with people who will push you, closer to mark of the prize of the high calling. Surround yourself with people who value themselves enough to live an upright life. Set standards for the people you allow in your life. Be sure those standards match your heavenly value. Be kind to others, and show love in all you do. Respect people as individuals and practice the golden rule daily. If you want to be valued, then value others. You teach people how to treat you. People will only do what you allow.

Be ambitious yet humble. Strive for greatness and don't place limits on yourself because the God you serve is limitless. Stays focused on your purpose, and remember where your blessings come from. Submit to God's plan for your life and the rest will follow. Do not seek recognition or praise from the world. Instead, seek to please God and the world will have no choice but to recognize the anointing on your life.

Most importantly, RISE! Rise up and take your rightful place as heirs to the throne of grace. Take these qualities and make them apart of who you are as a person. Live them daily in everything you do. Rise above the challenges and the discouragement. Spread your wings and FLY! Soar to the great heights that God intends to take you to. Live the abundant life he promised you.